BEARDS ...A SPOTTER'S GUIDE

C. FROST-SHARRATT

spruce

An Hachette UK Company

First published in Great Britain in 2010 by
Spruce, a division of Octopus Publishing Group Ltd
Endeavour House, 189 Shaftesbury Avenue, London, WC2H 8JY
www.octopusbooks.co.uk
www.octopusbooksusa.com

Copyright © Octopus Publishing Group Ltd 2010
Illustration copyright © Ben Swift

ISBN-13: 978-1-84601-359-1

A CIP catalogue record of this book is available from the British Library.

Printed and bound in China

10 9 8 7 6 5 4 3 2 1

Contents

Introducing the Beard

If you take a few minutes out of your day to look at your fellow shoppers, workers, passengers or pedestrians, you will probably be surprised by the number of beards on display. It is easy to ignore or overlook face fuzz, but once you've experienced the buzz of correctly identifying a set of whiskers, you'll start to notice beards in all sorts of weird and wonderful places.

The Evolution of Facial Hair

Men – and a limited number of follicularly enhanced ladies – have been growing beards since time immemorial. Cave dwellers had no choice in the matter and made do with un-sculpted mops of raggedy facial hair (although the benefits of warmth probably outweighed any hang-ups they had about their appearance).

However, as soon as razors, scissors and pomade were readily available, men personalized their appendages with wanton abandon. Different eras heralded the arrival of different styles, until there was such an array of beards to choose from that some order needed to be restored to the serious business of facial hair.

To arrest the onset of beardie chaos, some ground rules were put in place. Styles became grouped and categorized, and help was made available to facially fickle men, or those who needed guidance on growing, grooming and trimming techniques.

An Abundance of Beards

Today, if you keep your eyes peeled, you will be able to see examples of every style of beard. The intrepid whisker wearer has withstood ridicule, abuse, derision and exclusion over the years in order to flourish and multiply.

Long-lost beards have been reintroduced to the wild, and a careful nurturing of more popular styles has seen a resurgence of whiskers in previously barren beardie areas. This has brought much joy to beard spotters everywhere as they no longer need to search far and wide for an Octopus (see page 92) or sit outside a tattoo parlour all day hoping to catch a quick peek of an El Insecto (see page 90).

Beard spotting these days is much more of a sedentary pastime, and finally enthusiasts can dispense with the crampons, compasses and emergency food rations altogether. All but the rarest of beards can be seen from a decent vantage point in any supermarket car park - if you're prepared to put the hours in, that is.

The Beard Spotter's Secret Weapon

This book is a handy guide for the amateur beard spotter. You can fit it in your pocket and whip it out at a moment's notice when a tricky chin appendage wanders past.

Now, you'll never need to be embarrassed in the face of fuzz-wearers. With your new-found knowledge you will be able to quickly and easily identify all the major beard types. Best of all, you will learn their individual habitats, characteristics and breeding habits, so you will know if it's safe to approach the beard in question, or whether it's better to keep your distance.

With beardies inflicting their variously pruned and preened whiskers on the rest of the population, it seems only fair that the smooth-skinned among us should have some insider information. 'Forewarned is forearmed' as someone once said and this book will give you all the ammunition you need to inform and educate yourself about this curious group of men, united by their love of wearing whiskers.

On the Chin

This collection of beards remains the preserve of those who use their face fuzz to keep their chins warm. These styles are worn by everyone from the experimental toe-dipper in the world of beards, to the lifelong enthusiast.

Old Dutch

Latin Name *Stylus Eradicatus* **Family** On the Chin **Age Group** 40-70

This is the beard of the fashion-unconscious beard-maestro. He's an old-school shepherd or farm labourer who doesn't give a monkey's arse about what people think of him. Just as well really – those thoughts aren't complimentary.

Shape & Character...Bulbous beard that can be grown to epic proportions. Popular with erotic magazine subscribers and ferret fanciers. Old Dutch often has a sleepy eye and a roving hand.

Habitat...When he's finished shovelling manure on the farm, you'll find him at the front row of life-drawing classes or wandering around the lingerie section of department stores wearing a greasy raincoat. Home is the family hovel in Norfolk.

Breeding...Old Dutch will often remain a bachelor, though not for want of trying. Some members of the species do mate successfully, on condition that they breed purely for the purpose of offspring and then get separate bedrooms. This arrangement seems to suit both parties.

"My, what smooth skin you have. Would you like to nuzzle up to my Old Dutch?"

How
Common

%*@!
Factor

Pulling
Power

Hollywoodian

Latin Name *Homo Self-Importantus* **Family** On the Chin **Age Group** 30-45

This is a favourite amongst the acting or directing fraternity, but Hollywood itself is still a distant dream (and will probably remain so). They work largely on corporate videos and suburban pub-theatre plays.

Shape & Character...An even covering of chin and lip hair. Traditionally worn by anyone with a tenuous link to the movies, it is now a favourite amongst yummy daddies. The wearer will often look focused as he tries to multi-task: texting and pushing a swing at the same time.

Habitat...Hollywoodians congregate in the leafier parts of London. They hang around film sets like a bad smell and drink at any pubs that have celebrity connections. Home is a ramshackle Georgian house inherited from their grandparents.

Breeding...Dolly birds feature in the early life of the Hollywoodian, but these will be exchanged for a supermodel with brains as they get more serious in older age. They breed later in life and readily give up their badly paid jobs to ferry the kids between nursery and nanny.

"I find it really fulfilling being a stay-at-home dad. Once the nanny's left for the day, there's a whole hour of quality time."

How Common ●●●◐○

%*@! Factor ●●●◐○

Pulling Power ●●●●◐

Chin Strap

Latin Name *Yora Lucer* **Family** On the Chin **Age Group** 25-50

This beard is worn by everyone from wannabe DJs to cowboy landlords. They may look friendly enough, but prepare to exit quickly if they mention anything about pyramid selling schemes.

Shape & Character...Line of face fuzz that follows the contours of the chin. Popular among full-figured men with shady business contacts or slow-on-the-uptake janitors with nervous twitches and squeaky shoes.

Habitat...Chin Straps are rampant in fast-food outlets, where they use greasy fingers to tap on dated mobile phones. You'll also spot them in discount shopping outlets in Tyneside, trying to squeeze their substantial girths into polyester suits. They live with their ageing parents and numerous cats.

Breeding...Chin Straps love the ladies and they love them big style. They may fool around for a while but will settle on someone who knows her way around the bedroom and kitchen. Sexual harassment claims are common in later years when they try it on with random acquaintances.

"Give me a squeeze and I'll share my fries."

Fact!

'Beard' is a slang term for a cover-up partner, whose job is to conceal the other's sexual orientation.

How Common

%*@! Factor

Pulling Power

Goatee

Latin Name *Tickel Me Chinnius* **Family** On the Chin **Age Group** 20-60

People have a misconception that Goatees are all creative types. But rather than signing off million-dollar advertising budgets, they're probably sorting through junk mail in the post room or collecting glasses in the Student Union.

Shape & Character...Cropped tuft of chin fuzz. Popular with students shaking off parental shackles. Also, wannabe rock stars and graphic designers scrabbling around at the bottom of their respective career ladders. Wearers have a misplaced sense of self-worth and a fondness for the air guitar.

Habitat...The Job Centre is a regular haunt, as Goatees rarely find their ideal job...or any job for that matter. Home is a student cesspit in the rough end of town, regardless of age.

Breeding...Goatees have a specific mating ritual that involves pinpointing an unsuspecting lady, plying her with alcohol and compliments and then marrying her before she sobers up. Seedier ones try to pull their mates' divorced mums in order to move into a house with central heating.

"Of course, I could have been touring the world in a famous band but I wasn't prepared to give up my artistic integrity."

How
Common

%*@!
Factor

Pulling
Power

Petit Goatee

Latin Name *Ego Inflatus* **Family** On the Chin **Age Group** 25-50

The Petit Goatee is a rite-of-passage style for film runners and tea boys. This is an idler's beard — but the type of idler who carries a mirror and a breath-freshener spray in his pocket, just in case.

Shape & Character...Small sculpted beard. Wearers often work in achingly trendy fashion boutiques, where they sneer at customers. They like to give the impression of haughtiness, but their weekly wage wouldn't even buy them a pair of designer socks.

Habitat...You'll spot them in parks and cafés, reading books they don't understand. They also congregate in dark, dingy performance art clubs in Brighton - they avoid bright lights at night because the 5 o'clock shadow plays havoc with this beard style.

Breeding...Petit Goatees like to keep their options open and tend to switch locations just before a relationship looks in danger of developing into something serious. However, they always like to have a mate in tow, so they quickly swoop down on new prey in each territory.

"I just can't stop my fingers tapping when those groovy jazz beats kick in."

How Common

%*@! Factor

Pulling Power

Circle Beard

Latin Name *Commonus Mukus* **Family** On the Chin **Age Group** 18-50

He will insist that he's a yet-to-be-discovered songwriter or a struggling novelist, but you can be sure that he'll still be cleaning your windows or patching up your exterior paintwork in five years' time.

Shape & Character...An innocuous patch of hair with vague grooming criteria. Although favoured by tortured artistes, it's also the beard of choice for ageing surfers and charity collectors. And men with no qualms about scratching their balls in public.

Habitat...You'll often find Circle Beards lurking in coffee shops, where they nurse a tepid Americano and pretend to do important things on a laptop. They also hang out in south London builders' merchants and greasy spoons.

Breeding...Most Circle Beards mate for life. They generally shack up with the first lady who says 'yes' and, when they get bored with each other's company, they have kids. When they get bored with the kids, they get a dog and have dalliances with dim-witted dolly birds half their age.

"I'm only doing this until I get a publisher for my novel. I've written ten pages already."

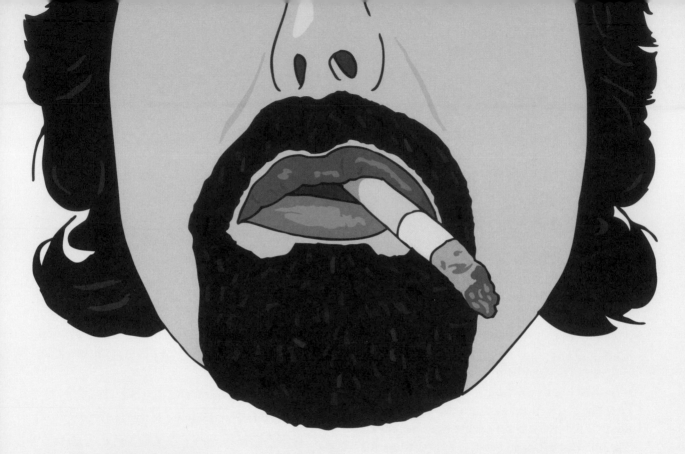

How Common
%*@! Factor
Pulling Power

Soul Patch

Latin Name *Organ Minusculus* **Family** On the Chin **Age Group** 25-50

The Soul Patch is the badge of honour for conceited university students. Also sported by musically minded layabouts who live with their mum and still have a racing-car duvet on their bed.

Shape & Character...Minuscule tuft of hair on a clean-shaven lower lip. The beard of choice for facial hair phobics and custom-car fanatics. The beard is often a reflection of the wearer: this is a man of diminutive proportions.

Habitat...The Soul Patch is a permanent fixture in second-hand record shops and impromptu jamming sessions in underground clubs in Bristol. Often seen sporting oversized headphones and nodding his head to obscure acid jazz tracks. Tends to stick to larger cities for better 'vibes'.

Breeding...Soul Patch attracts like-minded dreamy musos or aspiring writers who work in sandwich bars. They will get through a steady succession of identical-looking mates. Eventually, Soul Patch will hook up with the girl he fancied in primary school and put down a deposit on a flat in commuterville.

"Who needs food when there's music? I feed body and soul on creativity...and tomato-sauce sarnies."

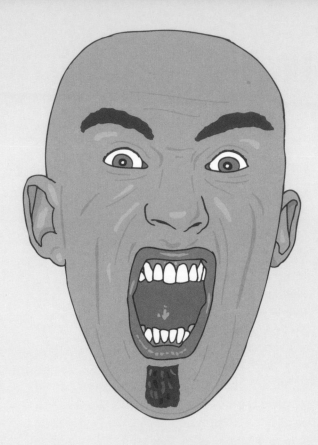

Fact!
Ironically, ZZ Top drummer, Frank Beard, is the only beardless band member!

How Common

%@! Factor*

Pulling Power

Chin Curtain

Latin Name *Homo Defunctus* **Family** On the Chin **Age Group** 25-50

Although this is traditionally a seafarer's beard, the Chin Curtain is now coming ashore and stepping onto dry land. It is sported by fashion-phobic born-again Christians, hairy naturists and college lecturers.

Shape & Character...Cropped beard that leaves the actual face free from whiskers. Obligatory chin wear for owners of decrepit fishing vessels and men who smoke pipes and see nothing wrong with wearing skimpy shorts, knee socks and sandals out in public.

Habitat...Chin Curtains spend their waking hours scuttling around the bowels of their land-locked boats in Great Yarmouth, trying out sailing knots or petting mangy dogs. Weekends are spent Morris dancing or mowing the grass in the buff.

Breeding...The boat helps to snare a fishwife and it also supplies a ready escape route from the inevitable nagging. The wily old Chin Curtain may be able to get his leg over with inquisitive hippy types if he doesn't let his personal hygiene fall by the wayside.

"I've scrubbed the anchor. Now it's time I anchored me a scrubber."

How Common

%@! Factor*

Pulling Power

The Full Monty

Ducktail

Garibaldi

Designer Stubble

Verdi

French Fork

Spade

Wizard

Short Boxed Beard

This next set of beards concentrates on fuller facial coverage. Although the beard length varies dramatically, wearers of these styles like to hide more of their face, or to draw attention away from it. Do we need to spell it out?

Ducktail (or Stiletto)

Latin Name *Nauticalus Prickus* **Family** The Full Monty **Age Group** 40-60

Commonly seen as slightly eccentric pub-quiz regulars or helpful old Scout leaders, Ducktails can be sly old foxes. Contrary to popular belief, they are often closet bigots with suspicious financial dealings and locked cellars.

Shape & Character...Neat, short beard. Popular among small-time UKIP supporters and Home Counties businessmen. The point intends to imply playful eccentricity but just means they can stroke themselves shamelessly in public.

Habitat...Found in middle management offices of data-processing companies or provincial estate agents. Tend to live on 1960s housing estates and socialize at the local yacht club. Proud owners of second-hand burgundy Jaguars and priceless collections of pastel cashmere jumpers.

Breeding...Ducktails attract a number of mates, including local-girl first wife, with whom children are likely. This is followed by a trophy wife in later life (coincides with boat purchase). Whilst he's in it for the looks, she's got her eye on his final-salary pension. Smattering of business-trip hookers.

"Ahoy there ladies, can I give you a hand with your buoyancy aids?"

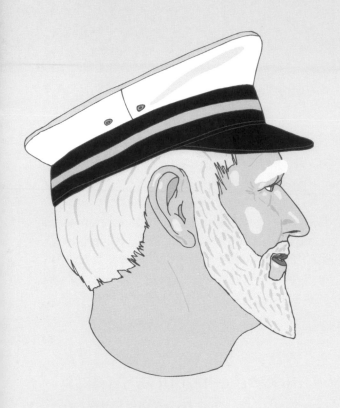

*How
Common* 🧔🧔🧔🧔⚪

%@!
Factor* 🧔🧔🧔⚪⚪

*Pulling
Power* 🧔🧔🧔🧔⚪

Garibaldi

 Latin Name *Whereis Facus* **Family** The Full Monty **Age Group** 40-70

Assumed to be lacking in the looks department due to the huge facial hair coverage. This fluffy appendage usually belongs to a hirsute hippy or gardener with severe personal hygiene issues.

Shape & Character...No trimming or pruning required for this face-eating beard. Popular with university professors, old-school hippies and pimply eco-warriors looking for a little gravitas.

Habitat...Common near airports with expansion plans, Somerset cider festivals and recitals of sea shanties. Work as cash-in-hand Santas in out-of-town shopping centres over the festive season. This beard is also a habitat in itself, providing a cosy home for small, furry animals.

Breeding...Garibaldis like to mate with equally hairy ladies and can sniff an unshaven armpit a mile off. He's a bit of a one-hit wonder in the bedroom, so regularly seeks out one-night stands with peace activists to add some variety to his mating ritual.

"Why wear deodorant? The natural smell of a sweaty woman is much more sensual."

How Common

%*@! Factor

Pulling Power

Designer Stubble

Latin Name *Crisis En Midageus* **Family** The Full Monty **Age Group** 20-50

Tries to impress by saying he's a property developer or model booker. Dig deeper and you'll discover he owns a maisonette in Lewisham and arranges flights for misguided girls to work in 'dance' clubs in the Med.

Shape & Character...A few days' facial hair growth. This beard is a sign of vanity or laziness, and he'll either be smothered in cheap aftershave or smell of stale sweat. He wears leather trousers and Cuban heels. Calls everyone 'babe'.

Habitat...Leaning out of his car window or loitering around the gym reception, ogling women. Lives in a state of disarray in a penthouse by the river....well, the top floor of an ex-council block in Lewisham.

Breeding...Family pressure leads him to marry quite young, but it rarely lasts. Relief on both sides results in an amicable split, and he starts spending well beyond his means on call-girls. Over the years, he has a couple of kids from one-night stands. In middle age, a shady wife tries to get his money.

"How much? Well I hope you make me breakfast in the morning as well for that price."

Fact!

Beard (verb): to seize or pluck someone's beard; to defy boldly (beard the lion in his own den).

How Common

%*@! Factor

Pulling Power

Verdi

Latin Name *Conflictus Stylus* **Family** The Full Monty **Age Group** 40-70

Sported by self-confessed opera buffs and wine bores. Behind closed doors they tend to be cantankerous old relics with a saucy postcard collection and a flatulence problem that borders on the obscene.

Shape & Character...Neatly groomed, separate beard and moustache. He puts a lot of effort into his facial hair, neglecting most other areas of his life. Borderline alcoholic and crossing the line between cuddly and obese.

Habitat...Obligatory attendance at Ascot Races and annual German beard-growing competitions. Makes a nuisance of himself at the local amateur theatre company, having failed an audition for *Hello Dolly!* 15 years ago. Lives in a crumbling stately pile in Berkshire.

Breeding...Played the field at Cambridge but settled down with a carefully vetted gal on graduation. When she's birthed, baked and bored herself to near delirium, he'll trade her in for a younger model. Indulges in role-play with dominatrix escorts while the second wife gets her hair done.

"I say, what a damn fine filly. Looks like a good breeder too. Ah, she's your daughter you say? Splendid, old chap."

How Common

%*@! Factor

Pulling Power

French Fork (or Byzantine Style)

Latin Name *Twatus Totalis* **Family** The Full Monty **Age Group** 20-50

This comedy beard implies the wearer has a sense a humour. However, he's actually sporting it as a badge of creativity during his years as a mediocre fashion student or a misunderstood street artist.

Shape & Character...Two-pronged attachment on the chin. Once cultivated, French Forks are loath to remove their whiskers. As such, you'll see the style on grungy looking middle-aged men who work as buskers or street cleaners.

Habitat...Often live with their parents in a Basingstoke semi until their mid-thirties. When the fashion career fails, they get jobs in fast-food outlets or pet supply warehouses. Weekends are spent at historical re-enactment clubs or metaphysical theory conventions.

Breeding...Thankfully, the odd appearance of the French Fork means that he is unlikely to have a bevy of female admirers. Rejected cult wannabes might be tempted while he still has his youth, but in later years he will resort to specialist dating agencies for prospective partners.

"Take me to your leader. What am I saying? I am your leader. Follow me to my den of iniquity."

How
Common

%*@!
Factor

Pulling
Power

Spade

Latin Name *Familium Tu Closum* **Family** The Full Monty **Age Group** 40-60

They might look like folk singers, but most Spades are between homes, between jobs or a few screws short of a toolbox. He's a man of few words...because he only knows a few words.

Shape & Character...Large, blunt beard. Commonly sported by misfits who collect rusty car parts and keep them in their front gardens. Often have facial ticks, dubiously stained trousers and bits of food festering in their beards.

Habitat...You will see them on park benches, where they shout at themselves and random passers-by. Also, driving tractors in remote areas of the West Country, usually accompanied by a feral dog. Home is a dilapidated cottage down a dirt track.

Breeding...The staring eyes ward off most potential partners. Occasionally, a buxom school matron with fantasies of being a farmer's wife is prepared to overlook the pungent aroma. When all else fails, there's always the livestock.

"Bath? I don't need a bath. I had one at Christmas!"

How
Common

%*@!
Factor

Pulling
Power

Wizard

Latin Name *Magicatum Neglectus* **Family** The Full Monty **Age Group** 50-70

This looks like the beard of an eccentric old inventor or environmentalist, but he's usually propping up the end of the bar, talking to himself and letting his dog drink from his pint glass.

Shape & Character...Facial hair with no boundaries. Seen on second-hand book dealers and ex-glam rock band members. The length is meant to imply virility but memory loss leads to shoddy grooming and an unpleasant smell.

Habitat...Clinging onto treetops near proposed motorway developments or tapping sandalled feet to folk bands at cider festivals. Occasionally spotted in chemistry labs in posh boarding schools in Surrey where he also lives - in a converted storage room.

Breeding...Wizards are quite successful in their younger years when they pull like-minded hippies with childbearing hips. More reclusive as they get older, relying on occasional flings with palm readers or batty school-dinner ladies.

"Just popping out for a pint of milk. Remind me where the shops are again...oh, and how much coinage will I need to buy said milk?"

How
Common

%*@!
Factor

Pulling
Power

Short Boxed Beard

Latin Name *Educator Tedium* **Family** The Full Monty **Age Group** 35-60

He's either a chemistry teacher or he works in an obscure council office processing useless data. This is the 'crazy' uncle who has Christmas jumpers and a collection of bad magic tricks.

Shape & Character...Short, closely cropped beard. It's the safe option – the beard equivalent of corduroy trousers or cocoa. He buys all his clothes from the back of Sunday supplements and doesn't leave home without a flask of tea plus a damp, clingfilm-wrapped cheese sandwich.

Habitat...Never happier than when he's writing in a notebook, so you'll often see him train or plane spotting. Otherwise, he'll be hiking in the Lake District, or attending model railway conventions.

Breeding...His monogamous persona attracts the ladies and he'll usually marry his university girlfriend. Affairs with sixth-form students during his teaching career can often land him in trouble, however. Paternity suits are not uncommon for wayward Boxes.

"Stay behind after class and I'll teach you all about glacial discharge."

How Common ●●●●○

%*@! Factor ●●○○○

Pulling Power ●●●●○

Mix 'n' Match

Fu Manchu
Franz Josef
A La Souvarov
Hulihee
Mutton Chops
Anchor
Balbo
Van Dyck (Classic)
Van Dyck (Modern)
Napoleon III Imperial
Friendly Mutton Chops
Handlebar & Goatee

These beards cater to the tastes of the indecisive whisker wearer. A motley assortment of random moustache and chin fluff - there's something here for everyone.

Fu Manchu

Latin Name *Drupus Apendum* **Family** Mix 'n' Match **Age Group** 30-50

Commonly mistaken for a playboy bachelor or an American drama series actor, this laid-back lothario tends to supplement his meagre salary with an unhealthy gambling habit.

Shape & Character...Long, droopy moustache. Career options range from call-centre worker to nightclub owner. Wearers are united by their vanity, and Fu buys his hair colour from the chemist and his sun-kissed skin tone from a Nottingham tanning shop.

Habitat...Tend to settle in mid-sized towns around the Midlands. Often seen wearing leather chaps in fetish clubs, or may be hanging around motorway service stations partaking in some mutual motorbike appreciation.

Breeding...Fu has a haphazard approach when it comes to mating, with a penchant for burlesque dancers and cocktail waitresses in his youth. Rarely gets married, though willing to take on his partners' kids. Selection of bikers and bikers' wives sees him through to old age.

"I'm a free spirit – I'm always free for a fit woman and I love spirits."

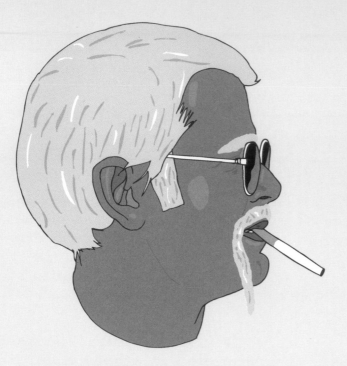

Franz Josef

Latin Name *Dominatum Pervus* **Family** Mix 'n' Match **Age Group** 30-60

The distinctive shape means he's often mistaken for a ship's captain or a headmaster. Look more closely, however, and you'll see a set of caretaker keys dangling from his belt.

Shape & Character...Bushy sideburns meet trimmed moustache. This split-personality beard appeals to authoritarians, musos teetering on the edge of failure and men with a cupboard full of well-used Victorian school canes.

Habitat...Dotted about provincial towns in Derbyshire and Lancashire, where he resides in a sixties cul-de-sac. When he's not curtain twitching he's loitering on the sidelines of military parades or reading the dirty bits in books he has no intention of buying.

Breeding...Usually a late developer with just a few fumbles to his name before he marries the mild-mannered secretary from his first office job. She does a runner when he suggests going to swingers' parties. Works his way through the 'masseurs' advertised in the local newsagent's.

"Fifty lashes today, I think, Chantelle – I've been a very naughty boy."

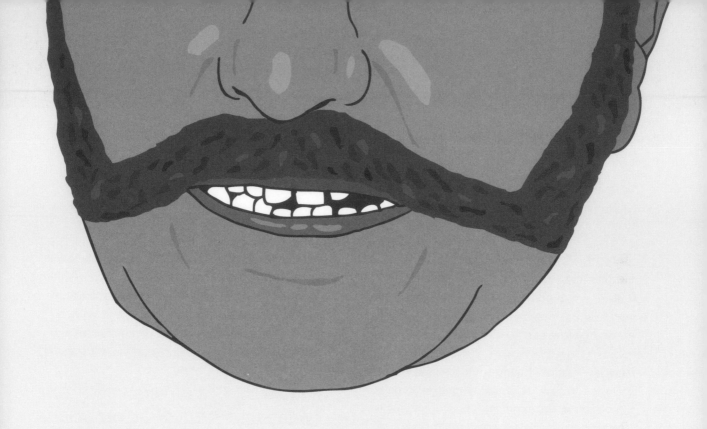

 How Common ◆ ◆ ◆ ◆

 %*@! Factor ◆ ◆ ◆ ◆

 Pulling Power ◆ ◆ ◆ ◆

A La Souvarov

Latin Name *Ironicus Idiatum* **Family** Mix 'n' Match **Age Group** 35-70

Worn to achieve a look of superiority or a military bearing, but the closest he's been to a war zone is when he went paintballing for a stag do.

Shape & Character...A hairy hairpin bend running from ear to ear. Popular with history buffs. Also, graphic designers who think they're being achingly cool and ironic but just look like extras in a low-budget Victorian drama.

Habitat...Lecture theatres and antique fairs are popular territory. They also pop up at jumble sales and charity shops, looking for unsoiled pantaloons and tweed jackets. Home is a poky flat with damp problems in Hove.

Breeding...Souvarov likes ladies who are almost as intelligent as he thinks he is: favourite pulling grounds are libraries and university canteens. Marries early but has numerous affairs with checkout girls and his wife walks out when she finds a barcode scanner in his underwear drawer.

"I just can't concentrate if I'm wearing a pair of boxer shorts that hasn't been ironed."

Fact!

It's rumoured that in the 1960s, the CIA looked at ways of ridding Fidel Castro of his iconic beard.

How Common

%@! Factor*

Pulling Power

Hulihee

Latin Name *Stickus Outus* **Family** Mix 'n' Match **Age Group** 50-70

This is the man you hold doors open for. He might look like a distinguished army hero, but he's often just an eccentric old codger with a toy soldier collection.

Shape & Character...A short, neat moustache paired with extremely long sideburns. Popular with Neighbourhood Watch coordinators, prolific sherry drinkers and self-opinionated military bores.

Habitat...Often seen prancing about the stage in a doublet and hose in amateur dramatic productions. Works in an ancient insurance firm in London before retiring to the Cotswolds. Here he spends his days smoking a pipe and discussing his bowel movements in great detail.

Breeding...Hulihees play it safe and marry a girl from good stock with a triple-barrelled name. Two or three children are standard. Likely to play away from home on insurance conferences but the marriage survives to keep up appearances. Tries it on with the au pair with laughable consequences.

"Of course my father's father's father was a decorated man. Or was it a decorating man?"

How Common ●●○○○

%*@! Factor ●●●○○

Pulling Power ●●●○○

Mutton Chops

Latin Name *Roughus Arsus* **Family** Mix 'n' Match **Age Group** 40-60

The facial hair uniform of the career farmhand or council refuse disposal operative. His comic-book habit might seem cool, but notice how he pronounces each syllable and follows the words with his index finger.

Shape & Character...Overgrown sideburns. Historically linked to country bumpkins...and not much has changed. Often works with animals, as they're on an equal intellectual footing and have similar attitudes to hygiene.

Habitat...Regularly seen singing Elvis songs at karaoke competitions in Margate. Works on a fruit farm in Kent or a stud farm in Sussex. Lives in a tumbledown terrace house by a dual carriageway.

Breeding...Muttons rarely find a partner for life. Mating involves quickies in barns with seasonal workers from the Continent who want to improve their English. Divorced barmaids occasionally take them on in latter years to save on handyman costs.

"I often sit and talk to the animals, I know they understand what I'm saying."

How Common 🧔🧔🧔🧔🧔

%@! Factor* 🧔🧔🧔🧔🧔

Pulling Power 🧔🧔🧔🧔🧔

Anchor

Latin Name *Floatus Boatus* **Family** Mix 'n' Match **Age Group** 20-40

This badge of academia can be misleading – he might look like an Oxford don but he probably works in an amusement arcade while completing an NVQ at night class.

Shape & Character...Neatly trimmed moustache and small, pointy beard. Worn by students and professors with equal fervour and self-importance. Care must be taken when waxing: a particularly hard point can result in nasty chest injuries when dozing off during lectures.

Habitat...Perusing the philosophy section in bookshops; drinking herbal tea in rancid student living rooms covered in Che Guevara posters; queuing up for benefits cheque. Lives anywhere with a sub-standard art college or an abundance of DSS bedsits.

Breeding...Shares bed with fellow students for dual purposes of warmth and mating. A lazy attitude to soul mate selection often leads to commune-style living with numerous partners. Eventually sheds moral values and settles down with capitalist landlady for some late child rearing.

"I'm totally into existentialism, man. Hang on, that's my cheese. Put it back in the fridge and go and buy your own bloody groceries."

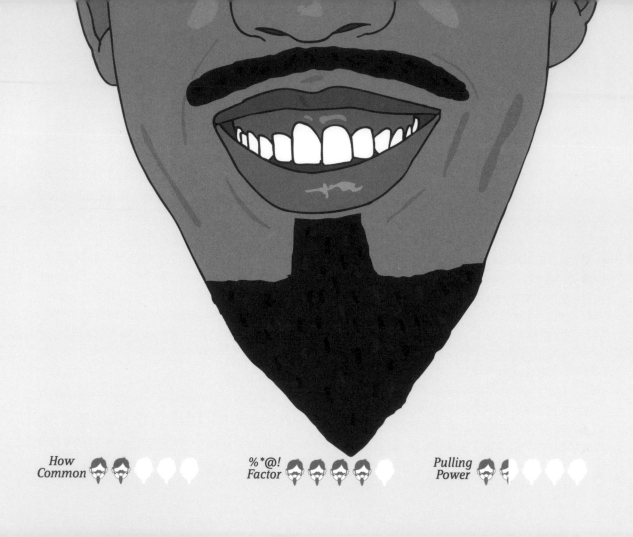

How
Common

%*@!
Factor

Pulling
Power

Balbo

Latin Name *Ego Maximus* **Family** Mix 'n' Match **Age Group** 25-45

Encourages the persona of being a harassed film director or a serious actor. In reality, this deluded beard only gets close to the camera when he's making tea for the second assistant sound recordist.

Shape & Character...Clipped moustache with longer chin appendage. This is the face fuzz of the out-of-work actor or the desperate Junior Ad Exec. Spends a lifetime slipping off the first rung of the career ladder.

Habitat...Hangs out in the gym to 'network' with other media losers. Afternoons spent wandering between Soho coffee shops, hoping to bump into real directors. Lives in a garret flat in Camden with someone who was once an extra on *EastEnders*.

Breeding...Surprisingly successful at mating, Balbos have perfected the art of sweet-talking young drama students into bed. When the age gap becomes too obvious, their steroid supplier introduces them to a female body builder looking for a sperm donor and marriage of convenience.

"Yeah, yeah, I had a look at the script but I'm just not sure I can make incontinence pads sound sexy."

How Common

%*@! Factor

Pulling Power

Van Dyck (Classic)

Latin Name *Arteus Farteus* **Family** Mix 'n' Match **Age Group** 20-50

He's got to be an intrepid explorer or an artist hasn't he? Well, if painting and decorating comes under the art category, then this is your man.

Shape & Character...Intricate combination of lip and chin hair. This beard needs attentive grooming, like its wearer's ego. Having failed as a portrait painter, he sulks at home in his studio (shed) doing occasional commissions for bereaved pet owners. Prone to tantrums.

Habitat...Needs space for creativity so lives in rural Devon. Hangs out in galleries in Totnes to slag off other people's work. Often seen handing business cards to anyone with a geriatric dog.

Breeding...Has early long-term relationship with free-spirited sprite. She flits off with a Turner Prize nominee so he marries a glum fellow artist. They barely speak and forego children on the grounds of pursuing their careers. Seduces life-drawing model for ongoing, casual affair.

"I think you'll agree that I've managed to capture Fido's carefree spirit perfectly."

Van Dyck (Modern)

Latin Name *Serialum Adulterus* **Family** Mix 'n' Match **Age Group** 30-50

He wants to be taken seriously, and the aviator glasses suggest he's a pilot or an Army Major. In fact, he's more likely to be a full-time software engineer with a remote-control plane and a penchant for khaki clothing.

Shape & Character...Three separate strips of facial hair that require precision grooming. Uses his wacky beard to compensate for his otherwise dull life. Colour blindness and an irrational fear of flying put paid to dreams of being a pilot, but he studies flight manuals on his daily commute.

Habitat...Works in London but lives in a semi on the outskirts of Croydon. Common in army surplus shops, military museums and at air shows. Can also be seen driving around in his camouflage Jeep.

Breeding...Modern Van Dycks have a misplaced perception of being heartthrobs and suffer many disappointments in early relationships. Tend to marry out of desperation and father children to follow the norm. Continually pester younger women and have occasional successes with bored housewives.

"When Armageddon happens, I'll be ready and waiting. The Jeep's stocked with everything you need to survive."

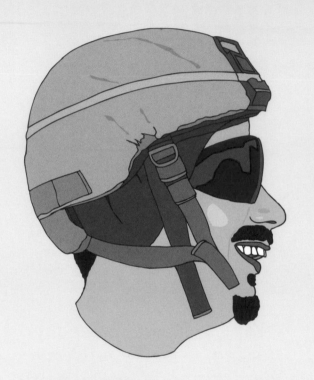

How Common

%@! Factor*

Pulling Power

Napoleon III Imperial

Latin Name *Whiskus Erectus* **Family** Mix 'n' Match **Age Group** 30-50

He gives the impression of having serious artistic intent, but it's hard to believe when you see him making sausage-dog balloons at children's parties.

Shape & Character...Three distinct points, all going in different directions. This whimsical beard is the calling card of the crazy sculptor or street artist with a sideline in timeshare sales and a wardrobe full of clown costumes.

Habitat...Commonly spotted in Leicester Square, where he draws caricatures of confused tourists or pretends to be a gold statue. Frequently hangs out in crusty old man pubs near his houseboat in the East End.

Breeding...Napoleon likes to woo the ladies in a traditional manner, with hand kissing and red roses. This works on drunk hen night attendees and daydreaming receptionists, but long-term partners can be elusive. Picks up single mums during stints as a children's entertainer.

"You are like a flower, my darling. I smelt your sweet perfume and I picked you from among the weeds."

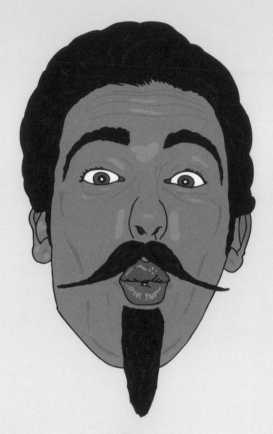

Fact!

In Ancient Egypt, kings and queens wore metal beards or 'postiches'. Look out for that comeback.

How Common

%@! Factor*

Pulling Power

Friendly Mutton Chops

Latin Name *Chinnus Chillius* **Family** Mix 'n' Match **Age Group** 30-60

He might look like a Neighbourhood Watch representative, but Friendly Mutton Chops is probably a crazed bird watcher or a flasher. He will literally bore you to death if you invite him into your house.

Shape & Character...Merger of overgrown moustache and shaggy sideburns: the beard of a lazy man who grows old disgracefully. He neglects his whole body, and his idea of exercise is opening non-branded cans of lager or doing crossword puzzles.

Habitat...Sipping real ale in crusty old pubs, tinkering with decrepit motorbikes in eye-wateringly tight leather trousers or making people's ears bleed with tuneless warbling at bluegrass music festivals.

Breeding...When the beard and the man are still in their prime, Friendly Muttons often snare an unsuspecting mate at Hell's Angels gatherings or 70s band tributes. As the beard gets unruly, she may have dalliances with smooth-skinned lovers, but Friendly Mutton will be blissfully ignorant.

"Bring me another beer, my little plum pudding. I don't want to miss the adverts."

How Common

%*@! Factor

Pulling Power

Handlebar & Goatee

Latin Name *Slyus Foxus* **Family** Mix 'n' Match **Age Group** 30-60

Ladies of a certain age swoon when they see this swashbuckling lothario, but he doesn't own the yacht – he's just a deckhand with a beady eye on their alimony payments.

Shape & Character...Goatee with a decorative moustache. Rite-of-passage beard for professional gigolos who stalk rich old ladies on the Med or rabbit-out-of-hat magicians who want to be taken seriously. Writes cringe-worthy poetry in his spare time; plucks his eyebrows and wears thongs.

Habitat...Can be seen targeting his prey in hotel piano bars and classy travel agents. Spends the summer in the south of France and winter in a static caravan in Dover.

Breeding...Series of holiday romances with French waitresses and cabaret performers. Occasionally pairs up for longer liaisons with yacht owners' discarded wives. If the money starts to run out, he might marry one of his rich, talcum powder-scented old ladies out of desperation.

"I love a woman with experience and class...and entitlement to free bus travel."

How Common

%*@! Factor

Pulling Power

Weird & Wonderful

These beards have the collective attribute of being just plain wrong. Some are barely there; others can be seen on satellite photos. They all act as a visual warning to steer well clear of the wearer.

GG

Latin Name *Minimatum Folicalus* **Family** Weird & Wonderful **Age Group** 35-50

So, he owns a boutique in north London. Did he mention that it's actually a kiosk selling phone cards? He's going for the hard-living look, but it's more along the lines of craggy street sleeper.

Shape & Character...Two neatly clipped ends of a moustache favoured by ageing rockers and unsuccessful fashion designers. GG is a vain man who swans through life convinced of his self-worth and has a skin thicker than a rhino's behind.

Habitat...He'll be at the front of every obscure punk-rock gig in Camden and then back home to his studio flat to drink absinthe shots until he passes out. Days are spent in pubs that smell of festering farts, or squatter-seized public buildings where he works on dire video-art installations.

Breeding...Tries to tempt drugged-up punk chicks back to his lair, but sobriety usually has them heading for the door in the morning. Sometimes hooks up with delusional performance artists looking for a new spin on their act. However, most liaisons begin with a cash handover and a sly wink from a hotel doorman.

"If it wasn't for the chicks, drugs and booze, I'd be a millionaire."

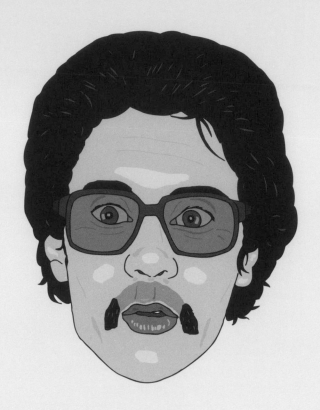

Fact!
Every US President from Lincoln to Wilson had beards save three: Johnson, McKinley, and Wilson himself.

 How Common

 *%*@! Factor*

 *Pulling Power*

Winnfield

Latin Name *Drugus Takus* **Family** Weird & Wonderful **Age Group** 30-50

He wants you to believe that he's peddling drugs and guns to Columbian street fighters, but he actually sells printer cartridges to small businesses.

Shape & Character...Clipped horseshoe-shaped moustache meets tidy lamb chops, as seen on wannabe pimps and porn stars with delusions of grandeur. He lives in a fantasy world and recites movie quotes to unimpressed mirrors.

Habitat...Common in Greater Manchester, where you'll see him strutting around in bad 70s suits. Winnfields divide their leisure time equally between the barbers, the betting shop and the all-you-can-eat noodle house.

Breeding...Winnfields don't like to put down roots and are likely to leave a trail of women and kids in various parts of the country. When there's nowhere left to run to, he might move in with his cinema-appreciation night-class teacher to re-enact famous sex scenes from American gangster flicks.

"I'm the man. I...am...the...man. I'm THE man. I'm the MAN."

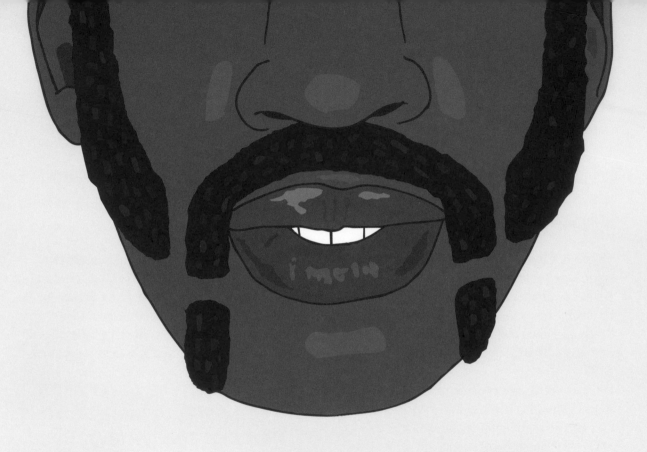

Tusks

Latin Name *Pointus Outus* **Family** Weird & Wonderful **Age Group** 40-65

People assume Tusks are tightrope walkers looking for a balance advantage in windy areas. However, they tend to earn their keep by claiming nominal prizes at beard-growing competitions.

Shape & Character...Two pruned and waxed beard side extensions. This man enjoys being the centre of attention and it's a style beloved by egocentric conductors and retired physicians. Keeps specimen trays as mementos of his career and walks through doorways at a strange angle.

Habitat...Tusks are two-a-penny in the cigar rooms of malodorous Mayfair gentlemen's clubs. Can also be seen nodding their appendages at classical music recitals or raking up leaves outside their Pimlico townhouses.

Breeding...Tusks marry and produce offspring at a young age, then adopt an attitude of casual indifference to spouse and children. Occasionally tempted into bed by sassy young viola players. Older age sees some Tusks bury their beards in a matronly bosom as they search for affection.

"Well I say...I've never heard... so you put it in there do you? Well that's jolly clever...and strangely pleasant."

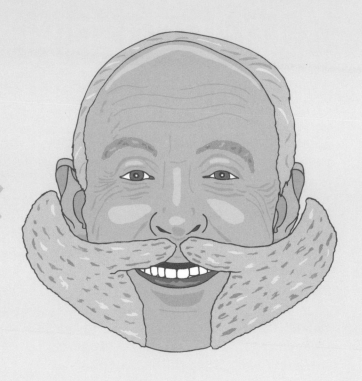

Fact!

Pogona and pogonia are kinds of 'bearded' lizard and orchid, from the Greek word 'pogon'.

How Common

%@! Factor*

Pulling Power

Rap Industry Standard

Latin Name *Tryus Tu Hardus* **Family** Weird & Wonderful **Age Group** 20-35

Likes to be known as a wannabe rapper or the local, small-time drugs dealer. In reality, he pawns his mum's china and gets high on energy drinks.

Shape & Character...A thin row of barely-there stubble. It's a statement beard, telling everyone who sees it that the wearer is a first-class tosser. The lightness of the beard is counteracted by the heavy assortment of cheap gold around his neck.

Habitat...The older R.I.S. hangs out in jewellery shops or lap-dancing clubs. Younger wearers are attached to a pitbull pup or a moody girlfriend with a Croydon facelift. Frequently seen in Walthamstow playing 'tunes' on stolen mobiles. Lives in a high-rise with his mum.

Breeding...He mates with a succession of young girlfriends and has more children than fingers before he's old enough to legally toast their births in the pub. Spends later years on the run from the benefits agency.

"Come and see my crib, ho. It's well tricked up with bling, innit?"

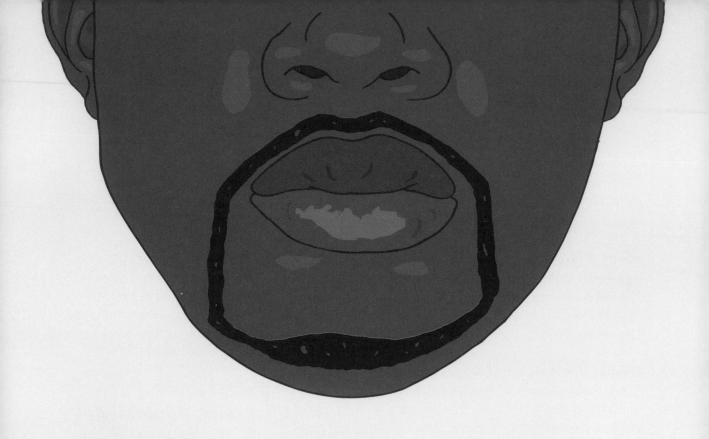

How Common

%*@! Factor

Pulling Power

Sparrow

Latin Name *Piratem Ridiculum* **Family** Weird & Wonderful **Age Group** 20-40

Sparrows give the impression of being achingly cool trendsetters. But, if you snoop around their minimalist loft apartment, you'll find school photos of an overweight, bespectacled youth with bad acne.

Shape & Character...A neat moustache with a long goatee that's divided and braided. This style is popular amongst musicians with over-inflated egos and 'wacky' media types with too much time on their hands.

Habitat...Sparrows don't like working for other people (and, let's face it, who'd employ them, looking like that?). You'll find them running dot-com start-ups or poncy hair salons in Shoreditch by day and drinking bottles of warm lager in 'trendy' bars by night.

Breeding...Sparrows can be surprisingly successful at attracting mates. However, they tend to believe in quantity not quality and are less fussy than other beards. Mating for life is a problem for them, with partners being changed more frequently than underpants.

"Yeah, I know (insert D-list celeb name) really well. We're totally on the same wavelength."

How
Common

%*@!
Factor

Pulling
Power

Avant-Garde Muso

Latin Name *Pantis Tu Titus* **Family** Weird & Wonderful **Age Group** 40-60

He might have been a real musician once, but these days he plays in a rock tribute band in community centres before serving up lunches for meals on wheels.

Shape & Character...This combination of a handlebar moustache and a trimmed Soul Patch is the facial adornment of musicians who never made the big time. Also stalker-style rock fans with pungent leather jackets and severe foot-tapping syndrome.

Habitat...Tend to migrate to the suburbs of northern cities, where they hang out in working men's clubs after putting in a day's work at the car parts factory. Karaoke contests always draw a big crowd of Musos, as do leather warehouse sales.

Breeding...Muso mates for life. Often marries his first long-term girlfriend after accepting they're both in love with an unobtainable 80s rock god. A couple of early planned children are often followed by an accidental third one in middle age. This injects a new lease of life into Muso man that can result in hair dying, crash dieting and a sordid affair.

"Rock is my religion, and I pray every day."

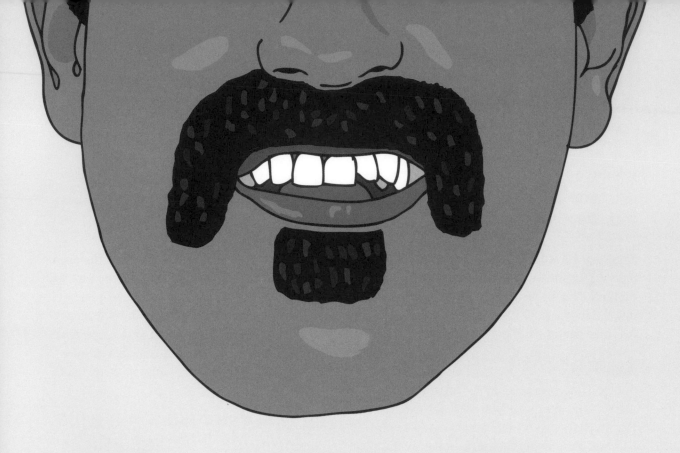

How Common

%*@! Factor

Pulling Power

Klingon

Latin Name *Weirdus Beardus* **Family** Weird & Wonderful **Age Group** 30-50

Likely to be a sci-fi enthusiast or a physics nerd, this is the man whose dull facts can quite quickly send you into a trance. A Klingon's list of hobbies always begin with the word 'amateur'.

Shape & Character...Facial hair grown to meet a moustache that isn't there. Popular with primary school teachers on a mission from a parallel universe. Takes over 'show and tell' with his collection of porcelain fantasy world figurines.

Habitat...Science fiction conventions see the largest gatherings of Klingons, but they also like to hang out in fancy-dress shops and the locations of suspected UFO sightings. Like to be home in their Surbiton new-builds by dusk.

Breeding...Their distinctive facial hair appeals to fantasy fans and they are likely to pair up with someone called Raven or Maiden while they're still in their prime. Role-play features heavily in the bedroom. Klingons believe in free love and will pick up oddball sci-fi fans at conventions around the world for brief flings in motel rooms.

"That's not fair – you wore the lamé jerkin and silver shoulder pads last time!"

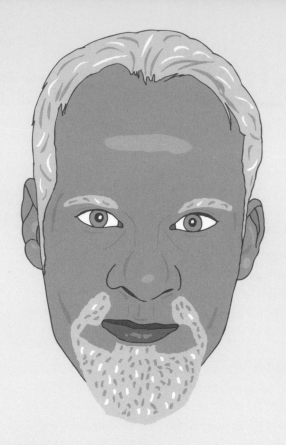

Fact!

Pogonion (noun): not a hairy vegetable served on hotdogs, but the forward-most part of the chin.

How Common

%*@! Factor

Pulling Power

Ho Chi Minh

Latin Name *Fakum Mysticalis* **Family** Weird & Wonderful **Age Group** 30-45

You could be mistaken for thinking he's a martial arts expert or a celebrity nutritionist, but the beard is misleading. If you're looking for a dial-a-life-coach or a dodgy gemstone dealer, he's your man.

Shape & Character...Moustache and goatee that is cultivated to lengthy proportions. The wearer delights in his aura of Oriental mysticism, but the closest he has been to China is his weekly takeaway of crispy duck.

Habitat...Having learnt the art of loafing on a gap year in San Francisco, he settles in Kensington, where he plies minted middle-aged women with New Age healing. Often seen leaving business cards at health clubs and riding around town on his Vespa.

Breeding...Has a string of American cheerleader girlfriends during his travels, followed by an earnest meeting of minds with his spiritual teacher back in the UK. Beds bored clients with talk of free love and emancipation then charges the illicit rendezvous as life-coaching sessions.

"The Kama Sutra is the true bible of enlightenment, Mrs Wenslydale-Smythe. We shall study it in great detail."

How
Common

%*@!
Factor

Pulling
Power

The Punk

Latin Name *Tuftus Prodit* **Family** Weird & Wonderful **Age Group** 20-35

He looks like a radical artist or hardcore punk fiend, but the beard is a cover-up: he still has a night-light in his bedroom and a bedtime glass of milk.

Shape & Character...Three carefully crafted, colourful beard prongs, sported by contemporary art students and members of bedroom punk bands. He's probably an ex-choirboy with an affected Cockney accent, rebelling against his strict boarding-school upbringing.

Habitat...Gather in packs around Trafalgar Square, where they pose for photos for intimidated Japanese tourists. Also found loitering in body-piercing parlours or at the benefits office. Home is a hushed-up suite of rooms in parents' palatial mock-Tudor mansion in Surrey.

Breeding...Early immersion in mating rituals, due to the boredom of boarding school, followed by a rebellious liaison with an unsuitable older woman. May settle down with fellow piercing fanatic, although embarrassing hospital trips are likely when metal adornments become entangled.

"I say, I am rather enjoying this ruby murray. Better slow up on the old lager though, or I'll be Brahms and Liszt."

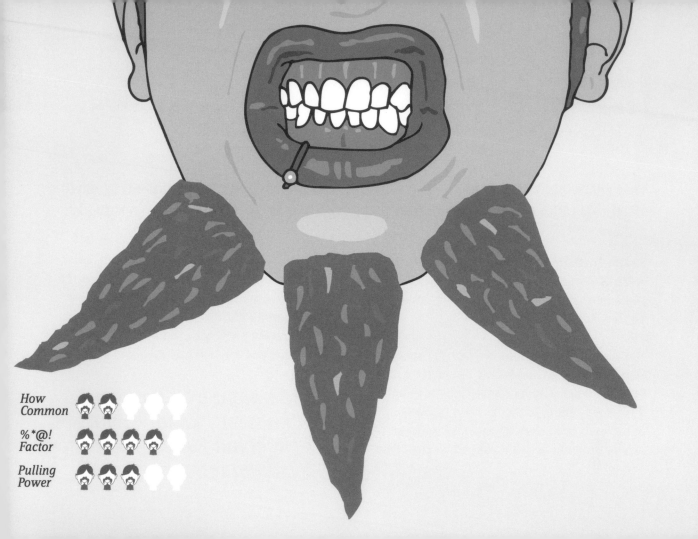

How Common

%*@! Factor

Pulling Power

El Insecto

Latin Name *Comrades No Havus* **Family** Weird & Wonderful **Age Group** 20-35

This crazy club DJ mashes up the dance floor all night before heading off to peel vegetables in a care-home kitchen. He has one beard prong for each personality.

Shape & Character...Two highly stylized tufts of hair. Worn by attention-seeking party animals and amateur fire-eaters. Penchant for tartan trousers and glow sticks.

Habitat...Run-down seaside resorts are popular stomping grounds and he can be spotted gurning in the chill-out room of trance clubs or spinning the disks at under-18 discos. Lives in Eastbourne in his nan's bungalow but spends evenings driving around town in a pimped-up Fiat Punto.

Breeding...As a gangly youth, El Insecto has to make do with dating the class nerd. Later on, his facial hair helps him attract dreadlocked ravers. May live with Earth Mother in a caravan. Settles down with the owner of a 'herbal highs' website, but smokes and swallows all the profits.

"Hi man, it's DJ Razor here. You know, DJ Razor? Yeah, OK it's Nigel but I wish you'd stop calling me that, man."

Want to scare people? Get those mandibles moving! Train them to grip stationery, sandwiches, or a bottle of beer...

How Common

%*@! Factor

Pulling Power

Octopus

Latin Name *Gloriatum Imbecilus* **Family** Weird & Wonderful **Age Group** 50-70

This looks like the facial hair of a yogi in training or a mad professor. He really is mad and has to sleep sitting up to avoid snapping his sculpted beard.

Shape & Character...Long, twirly fronds that resemble tentacles. This rare beard is reserved for the faces of theoretical physicists and sole survivors of 1970s hallucinogenic drug experiments.

Habitat...Octopi can be sighted at festivals, where they'll be throwing weird 'shapes' to psychedelic trance tunes. When the weather turns, they hunker down in meditation centres in the Scottish Highlands, where they park up their campervans and go foraging for wild mushrooms and berries.

Breeding...The man takes after his beard in this instance, and he never seems to have enough arms to grope and pinch unsuspecting ladies. Spends most of his life as a pervy batchelor, lying in wait for a gullible squeeze of a supply teacher sporting cankles and orthopaedic sandals.

"No, that's not dirt under my fingernails, it's the physical manifestation of subsistence living."

How Common

%@! Factor*

Pulling Power

Longboat

Latin Name *Nil Shamus* **Family** Weird & Wonderful **Age Group** 50-70

He has the demeanour and the beard of an ex-military man, but don't be deceived by the whiskers: he's a professional idler with a roving eye and a liking for the whisky bottle.

Shape & Character...A pair of mutton chops with extra length. The style is often accidental and therefore common amongst men suffering from memory loss. Also popular with doormen, butlers and old-money wastrels.

Habitat...With little to keep him occupied, Longboat often whiles away the morning in the library, reading free newspapers. He's a home-counties man through and through, and the sex shops of Berkshire are well used to him browsing the discount shelves.

Breeding...Longboats have a reputation for being serial husbands. He begins with a sensible, timid girl who pops out a few kids. When she's past her best, he places fruity ads in lonely-heart columns and attracts cash-strapped ladies with expensive tastes. He returns to a younger model in older age.

"Do you have any swimwear photos you could send me? I like to know that a lady has fashion sense before a date."

About the Author

C. Frost-Sharratt is a freelance features writer and a long-time beard spotter with a short fuse. When she isn't being wound up by facial hair, Cara writes features on entertainment, lifestyle and travel for a variety of pop-culture publications, both online and in print. She has still never found a bearded bloke who wouldn't benefit from a shave and a good, stern talking-to.

About the Illustrator

Camberwell graduate **Ben 'Swift' Reilly** is a Cambridge-based freelance illustrator. Under the guise of *Nonsinthetik* he creates fresh, colourful and often humorous artwork for a variety of music, fashion and publishing brands.

Acknowledgements

Publisher: Sarah Ford

Managing Editor: Camilla Davis

Editorial Assistant: Kate Fox

Designer: Eoghan O'Brien

Illustrator: Ben Swift

Production: Caroline Alberti